O9-AIE-344

Design: Judith Chant and Alison Lee

Recipe Photography: Peter Barry

Jacket and Illustration Artwork: Jane Winton, courtesy of Bernard Thornton Artists, London

Editor: Josephine Bacon

CHARTWELL BOOKS
a division of Book Sales, Inc.
POST OFFICE BOX 7100
114 Northfield Avenue
Edison, NJ 08818-7100

CLB 4265

Printed and bound in Singapore

ISBN 0-7858-0234-7

THE LITTLE BOOK · OF ·

Italian Cooking

An illustrated, step-by-step guide to classic Italian cooking.

CHARTWELL BOOKS, INC.

Introduction

Italian cooking is redolent of the warmer climes of the Mediterranean. It is bursting with the flavors and colors indigenous to Italy. Sun-drenched tomatoes are a common ingredient, as are the herbs of the Tuscan hills such as rosemary, basil, and oregano. Onions and garlic give a wonderful aroma and depth to many dishes. Cheese is an essential ingredient and is usually melted over the top of a dish. Olive oil is quite indispensable, and Italian wines, too, feature in lots of meat dishes as well as in desserts. In this collection of recipes, the Sicilian dessert wine, Marsala, makes several appearances as it particularly complements turkey, veal, and chicken. To obtain the authentic Italian flavor in these recipes, it is important to try to collect together all the exact ingredients specified.

The structure of an Italian meal is an interesting study in itself. An antipasto often starts the meal. This consists of a light appetizer, rather than a substantial course. Cold meats, fish, vegetables and salads, sometimes raw, sometimes lightly cooked, are all possible examples. Spinach Gnocchi would be served as an antipasto, and even pizza can fit into this category, although it is usually served as an entrée by non-Italians. Soup, or a pasta or rice dish follows the antipasto. These, of course, can also be

served as meals in themselves. This book features an excellent Minestrone recipe, and delicious examples of fresh pasta dishes, as well as a risotto.

With its extensive coastline – right down the "boot" and up again – Italy is naturally a nation of fish eaters. Anchovies frequently put in an appearance, as does red mullet – a delicate Mediterranean fish with a slight taste of shrimp. Veal and pork are favorite meats, chicken and turkey are also eaten, and beef is popular, too, in the north of the country. The piece of fish or meat that follows the soup, pasta or rice is typically embellished with herbs, mushrooms, cheese, tomatoes or garlic but is often served alone without accompanying vegetables. An example of this is Veal Scaloppini with Prosciutto and Cheese. A light dessert may follow, but these tend to be reserved for special occasions.

Whether it's a mouthwatering dessert, a traditional pasta bake or a stylish seafood dish, Italian cooking is a celebration of the best food the land has to offer, and with many of these ingredients now readily available in this country it is easy to bring a taste of Italy into your cooking. The recipes given here, with-their easy-to-follow, step-by-step instructions, give the cook a foolproof introduction to the summery taste of Italy.

Minestrone

SERVES 8-10

Everyone's favorite Italian soup doesn't always have to contain pasta. Ours substitutes potatoes and is hearty enough to serve as a one-pot meal.

PREPARATION: 20 mins
COOKING: 2 hours

1 cup navy or Great Northern beans
2 tbsps olive oil
1 large ham bone, preferably prosciutto
1 onion, chopped
2 cloves garlic, crushed
4 sticks celery, sliced
2 carrots, diced
1 small head Savoy cabbage or 6 cups fresh spinach, well washed
½ cup green beans, cut into 1-inch lengths
2 cups tomatoes, skinned, seeded, and diced
1 dried red chili
3 quarts water (or half beef broth, half water)
1 sprig fresh rosemary
1 bayleaf
3 potatoes, peeled, and cut into small dice
3 zucchini, trimmed and cut into small dice
1 tbsp minced basil
1 tbsp minced parsley
Grated Parmesan cheese

1. Place the beans in a large bowl, cover with cold water, and leave to soak overnight.

2. Heat the oil in a large pot or Dutch oven, and add ham bone, onion, and garlic. Cook until the onion has softened but not colored. Add the celery, carrots, cabbage, and green beans. If using spinach, reserve until later.

Step 1 Soak the beans overnight in enough cold water to cover.

3. Drain the beans and add them to the pot with the tomatoes and the chili. Add the water and bring to the boil, skimming the surface as necessary. Add the rosemary and bayleaf, and simmer, uncovered, for about 1¼ hours, or until the beans are tender.

4. Add the potatoes and cook a further 20 minutes.

5. Add the zucchini and spinach, if using, and cook, skimming the surface for about 20 minutes longer. Remove the ham bone, rosemary and bayleaf. Add the basil and parsley and adjust the seasoning. Serve with Parmesan cheese.

Bruschetta with Tomatoes

SERVES 6-8

Cooked over a wood fire in the traditional way, or more conveniently in the oven, tomatoes, basil, and crisp bread make an unusual and informal appetizer.

PREPARATION: 15 mins
COOKING: 25 mins

18 slices of crusty Italian bread, cut 1-inch thick
4 cloves garlic, crushed
⅔ cup olive oil
Salt and pepper
4-5 ripe tomatoes, depending on size
18 large fresh basil leaves

1. Place the bread slices on a baking sheet and toast for about 10 minutes on each side in a preheated 375°F oven.

Step 2 Spread some of the crushed garlic on each side of the toasted bread slices.

Step 3 Pour the warmed olive oil over the bread.

2. Spread some of the garlic on both sides of each slice.

3. Heat the oil gently in a small saucepan. Arrange the bread on a serving plate and immediately pour the warmed oil over it. Sprinkle with salt and pepper.

4. Slice the tomatoes into ½-inch thick rounds. Place one basil leaf and one slice of tomato on each slice of bread and serve immediately.

Spinach Gnocchi

SERVES 4-6

Gnocchi are little dumplings that are served like pasta. A dish of gnocchi can be served as an appetizer or as a light entrée, sprinkled with cheese or accompanied by a sauce.

PREPARATION: 15 mins
COOKING: 20 mins

2 cups chopped, frozen spinach, defrosted
1 cup ricotta cheese
⅓ cup Parmesan cheese
Salt and pepper
¼ tsp freshly grated nutmeg
1 egg, slightly beaten
3 tbsps butter

Step 3 Using floured hands, shape the gnocchi mixture into ovals, using about 1 tbsp mixture for each.

1. Press the spinach between two plates to extract all the moisture.

2. Mix the spinach with the ricotta cheese, half the Parmesan cheese, salt, pepper, and nutmeg. Gradually add the egg, beating well until the mixture holds its shape.

Step 5 Remove the cooked gnocchi from the pan with a slotted spoon, and place in a well-buttered ovenproof dish.

3. With floured hands, shape the mixture into ovals using about 1 tbsp mixture for each.

4. Lower the gnocchi into simmering water, 3 or 4 at a time, and allow to cook gently until they float to the surface, about 1-2 minutes.

5. Remove with a slotted spoon and place in a well-buttered ovenproof dish.

6. When all the gnocchi are cooked, sprinkle with the remaining Parmesan cheese and dot with the remaining butter.

7. Reheat 10 minutes in an oven preheated to 400°F, and brown under a preheated broiler before serving.

Fresh Pasta with Garlic and Parsley

SERVES 4

Cooked fresh pasta served in butter, olive oil, garlic, and parsley sauce makes a very simple but delicious meal.

PREPARATION: 5 mins
COOKING: 15 mins

1 pound fresh pasta
¼ cup butter
2 cloves garlic, minced
Few drops of olive oil
2 tbsps minced parsley
Salt and pepper

1. Cook the pasta to your liking in salted,

Step 2 Melt the butter in a skillet, add the garlic, and fry 1 minute.

Step 3 Add the drained pasta to the pan, stirring well to mix in the garlic.

boiling water. Rinse in hot water and set aside to drain.

2. Melt the butter in a skillet, add the garlic and fry 1 minute.

3. Add the drained pasta to the pan, stirring well to mix in the garlic. Cook for a few minutes.

4. Add a few drops of olive oil to the pan, remove from the heat, and sprinkle with the parsley. Season with salt and pepper and serve.

Chicken Cacciatore

SERVES 4-6

The use of herbs, wine, and vinegar in this delicious Italian family meal gives a wonderful, hearty flavor. Serve with rice or pasta, and a mixed salad.

PREPARATION: 30 mins
COOKING: 1 hour

---

4 tbsps olive oil
3 pounds chicken pieces
2 onions, sliced
3 cloves garlic, crushed
2 cups button mushrooms, quartered
⅔ cup red wine
1 tbsp wine vinegar
1 tbsp minced parsley
2 tsps chopped fresh oregano
2 tsps chopped fresh basil
1 bayleaf
4 cups canned tomatoes
⅔ cup chicken broth
Salt and freshly ground black pepper
Pinch of sugar

---

1. In a large skillet heat the oil and add the chicken pieces, skin side down, in one layer.

2. Brown 3-4 minutes, then turn each piece over. Continue turning the chicken portions until all surfaces are well browned.

3. Remove the chicken portions to a plate and keep warm.

4. Add the onions and garlic to the oil and chicken juices in the skillet. Cook lightly 2-3 minutes, or until they are just beginning to brown.

Step 2 Brown the chicken pieces 3-4 minutes then turn over to brown the other side.

5. Add the mushrooms to the pan and cook about 1 minute, stirring constantly.

6. Pour the wine and vinegar into the pan and boil rapidly to reduce to about half the original quantity.

7. Add the herbs, bayleaf, and tomatoes, stirring well to break up the tomatoes.

8. Stir in the chicken broth, and season with salt, pepper and sugar.

9. Return the chicken to the tomato sauce and cover with a tight-fitting lid. Simmer about 1 hour, or until the chicken is tender.

Veal Scaloppini with Prosciutto and Cheese

SERVES 4

Veal is the meat used most often in Italian cooking. Good veal is tender and quick cooking, but expensive. Save this recipe for your next dinner party!

PREPARATION: 15 mins
COOKING: 20 mins

8 veal scallops
2 tbsps butter or margarine
1 clove garlic, crushed
8 slices prosciutto
3 tbsps sherry
⅔ cup beef broth
1 sprig rosemary
8 slices mozzarella cheese
Salt and pepper

1. Pound the veal scallops out thinly between two pieces of parchment paper with a steak hammer or a rolling pin.

2. Melt the butter or margarine in a skillet and add the veal and garlic. Cook until the veal is lightly-browned on both sides.

3. Place a piece of prosciutto on top of each piece of veal and add the sherry, broth, and a sprig of rosemary to the pan. Cover the pan and cook the veal for about 10 minutes over gentle heat or until tender and cooked through.

4. Remove the meat to a warmed, heatproof serving platter and top each piece of veal with a slice of cheese.

Step 3 Place a slice of prosciutto on top of each veal slice. Pour the sherry and broth over the meat, and add the rosemary.

5. Bring the cooking liquid from the veal to the boil, season, and allow to boil rapidly to reduce slightly.

6. Meanwhile, broil the veal to melt and brown the cheese. Remove the sprig of rosemary from the sauce and pour the sauce around the meat to serve.

Step 6 Broil the meat to melt the cheese and lightly brown the top.

Mullet with Herb & Mushroom Sauce

SERVES 4

Mullet is a Mediterranean fish with a slight taste of shrimp. It is often cooked with the liver left in. If it is unavailable, use grouper, red snapper or redfish.

PREPARATION: 30 mins
COOKING: 25 mins

---

4 cups small mushrooms, left whole
1 clove garlic, finely chopped
3 tbsps olive oil
1 tbsp minced parsley
2 tsps finely chopped basil
1 tsp finely chopped marjoram or sage
Juice of 1 lemon
4 tbsps dry white wine mixed with ½ tsp cornstarch
Few drops anchovy extract
4 mullet, each weighing about 8 ounces
2 tsps white bread crumbs
2 tsps freshly grated Parmesan cheese

---

1. Combine the mushrooms, garlic, and olive oil in a small skillet. Cook over moderate heat about 2 minutes until the garlic and mushrooms are slightly softened. Add all the herbs, lemon juice, and white wine and cornstarch mixture. Bring to the boil and cook until thickened. Add anchovy extract to taste. Set aside while preparing the fish.

2. To clean the fish, cut along the stomach from the gills to the vent, the small hole near the tail. Clean out the cavity of the fish, leaving the liver, if desired.

Step 3 Lift the flap over the gills and use kitchen scissors to snip the gills away.

3. To remove the gills, lift the flap and snip them out with a sharp pair of scissors. Rinse the fish well and pat dry.

4. Place the fish, head to tail, in a shallow ovenproof dish that can be used for serving. The fish should fit snugly into the dish.

5. Pour the prepared sauce over the fish and sprinkle with the bread crumbs and Parmesan.

6. Cover the dish loosely with aluminum foil and cook in a preheated 375°F oven, about 20 minutes. Uncover for the last 5 minutes, if wished, and raise the temperature slightly to lightly brown the fish.

Tuscany Beef

SERVES 4

Beef gently cooked in red wine and flavored with rosemary and tomato makes a delicious casserole.

PREPARATION: 10 mins
COOKING: 2 hours

2 pounds chuck steak, cut into cubes
Flour for dredging
3 tbsps olive oil
1 clove garlic, chopped
½ tsp chopped rosemary
2½ cups red wine
2 tbsps tomato paste
Salt and pepper

1. Toss the meat cubes in the flour.

2. Heat the oil in a flameproof casserole. Add the garlic, meat, and rosemary. Fry on all sides until the meat is well-browned.

3. Deglaze the casserole with the red wine and then add in enough water to cover the meat.

4. Stir in the tomato paste, season with salt and pepper, cover and simmer gently about 2 hours. Check the meat for tenderness and remove from the heat when cooked through. Serve hot with plain boiled rice.

Pasta with Bolognese Sauce

SERVES 4

A rich, meaty sauce, cooked with white wine, carrot, onion, and tomatoes.

PREPARATION: 15 mins
COOKING: 50 mins

2 tbsps olive oil
1 carrot, finely diced
1 onion, finely diced
½ cup white wine
3 cups ground beef
½ cup water
3 tomatoes, skinned, seeded, and chopped
1 bayleaf
Salt and pepper
1 × 14-ounce package dried pasta
¼ cup butter

1. Heat the olive oil in a casserole and sauté the carrot and onion until nicely browned.

Step 1 Sauté the diced carrot and onion in the olive oil until nicely browned.

Step 3 Add the ground beef to the pan and cook to brown evenly.

2. Add the white wine and cook until the wine has completely evaporated.

3. Add the beef to the casserole and cook 2 minutes, stirring well to brown evenly.

4. Pour the water into the casserole, and add the tomatoes and the bayleaf. Season with salt and pepper, stir well, and cook over a gentle heat for a further 30 minutes.

5. About halfway through the cooking time for the sauce, set the pasta to cook in a pan of salted, boiling water until "al dente", following manufacturer's recommended cooking times. Rinse the pasta and allow it to drain well.

6. Melt the butter and stir it into the pasta then pour the sauce over them and serve immediately. Serve piping hot.

Veal with Marsala Sauce

SERVES 4

If you cannot get almond-flavored Marsala, use 3 tbsps Marsala and 1 tbsp Amaretto.

PREPARATION: 10 mins
COOKING: 1 hour

3 tbsps oil
1 large onion, finely sliced
2 pounds shoulder of veal, cut into cubes
4 tbsps almond-flavored Marsala
1 sprig rosemary
1 cup sliced mushrooms
Salt and pepper

1. Heat 2 tbsps of the oil in a large skillet or a flameproof casserole and sauté the onion and meat until sealed all over and nicely browned.

Step 1 Sauté the onion and veal in the oil until the meat is sealed and browned.

Step 2 Add the Marsala to the pan and deglaze.

2. Deglaze the pan with the Marsala and add sufficient water to completely cover the meat.

3. Add the rosemary to the pan, season with the salt and pepper, and simmer gently 45-50 minutes or until the meat is tender and the sauce has reduced and thickened.

4. Heat the remaining oil in a small skillet, and add the mushrooms. Sauté over medium heat. Sprinkle the veal with the chopped sautéed mushrooms before serving.

Pizza with Peppers, Olives, & Anchovies

SERVES 4

Pizza really needs no introduction. It originated in Naples and has been adopted everywhere. Change the toppings to suit your taste.

PREPARATION: 45 mins
COOKING: 20 mins

Pizza Dough
½oz fresh yeast or 1 package dry yeast
½ tsp sugar
¾ cup lukewarm water
2 cups all-purpose flour
Pinch of salt
2 tbsps oil

Tomato Sauce
2 tsps olive oil
1 onion, finely chopped
1 clove garlic, crushed
4 cups canned tomatoes
1 tbsp tomato paste
½ tsp each oregano and basil
1 tsp sugar
Salt and pepper

Topping
½ cup mozzarella cheese, grated
2 tbsps grated Parmesan cheese
½ each of red and green bell pepper, sliced
4 tbsps black olives, pitted
1 small can anchovies, drained

1. Cream the yeast with the sugar in a small bowl. Add the water and leave to stand 10 minutes.

2. Sift flour and salt into a bowl, make a well in the center, add the oil and the yeast mixture. Beat the liquid in the well, gradually incorporating the flour until it forms a firm dough.

3. Turn the dough out onto a floured surface and knead 10 minutes or until smooth and elastic. Place in a lightly-oiled bowl, cover with plastic wrap and leave to stand in a warm place 30 minutes, or until doubled in bulk.

4. Punch the dough down and knead it into a smooth ball. Flatten the dough and roll out on a floured surface into a 10-inch circle.

5. To prepare the tomato sauce, heat the oil in a heavy-based saucepan and add the onion and the garlic. Cook until softened but not colored. Add the remaining sauce ingredients.

6. Bring to the boil and then allow to simmer, uncovered, to reduce. Stir occasionally to prevent sticking. When the sauce is thick and smooth, leave it to cool.

7. Spread the cooled sauce over the pizza dough. Sprinkle half the cheese over the tomato sauce and then add the remaining topping ingredients. Sprinkle with remaining cheese and bake in a preheated 400°F oven 15-20 minutes or until the cheese is bubbling and the crust is brown.

Liver Veneziana

SERVES 4-6

As the name indicates, this recipe originated in Venice. The lemon juice offsets the rich taste of liver in this very famous Italian dish.

PREPARATION: 10 mins
COOKING: 30 mins

Risotto
3 tbsps butter or margarine
1 large onion, chopped
1 cup Italian (short-grained) rice
4 tbsps dry white wine
2½ cups chicken broth
¼ tsp saffron
Salt and pepper
2 tbsps grated fresh Parmesan cheese

Liver
2 tbsps butter or margarine
2 tbsps oil
3 onions, thinly sliced
1 pound calves' or lambs' liver
Flour for coating
Juice of ½ lemon
1 tbsp chopped parsley
Salt and pepper

1. Melt the butter for the risotto in a large skillet. Add the onion and cook until soft but not colored, over gentle heat.

2. Add the rice and cook about a minute or until the rice looks transparent.

3. Add the wine, broth, saffron, and seasoning. Stir well and bring to the boil. Reduce the heat and cook gently about 20 minutes, stirring frequently, until the liquid has been absorbed.

Step 3 Cook the risotto gently 20 minutes, or until the liquid has been absorbed.

4. Meanwhile, heat the butter and 1 tbsp of the oil for the liver in a large skillet, and cook the onions until golden.

5. Trim the liver and cut into strips. Toss in a sieve with the flour to coat.

6. Remove the onions from the skillet to a plate. Add more oil if necessary, increase the heat under the pan, and add the liver. Cook, stirring constantly, about 2 minutes.

7. Return the onions to the skillet, and add the lemon juice and parsley. Cook a further 2 minutes or until the liver is tender. Season with salt and pepper and serve with the risotto.

8. To finish the risotto, add the cheese and salt and pepper to taste when the liquid has been absorbed, and toss to melt the cheese.

Turkey Marsala

SERVES 4

Marsala is a dessert wine from Sicily which also complements turkey, veal, or chicken surprisingly well.

PREPARATION: 25 mins
COOKING: 15 mins

---

4 turkey scallops or breast fillets
¼ cup butter or margarine
1 clove garlic
4 canned anchovy fillets, drained and soaked in milk
4 slices mozzarella cheese
Capers
2 tsps chopped marjoram
1 tbsp chopped parsley
3 tbsps Marsala
⅔ cup heavy cream
Salt and pepper

---

1. If using the turkey breasts, flatten between two sheets of damp parchment paper with a steak hammer or rolling pin.

2. Melt butter in a skillet and, when foaming, add the garlic and the turkey. Cook for a few minutes on each side until lightly browned. Remove them from the pan.

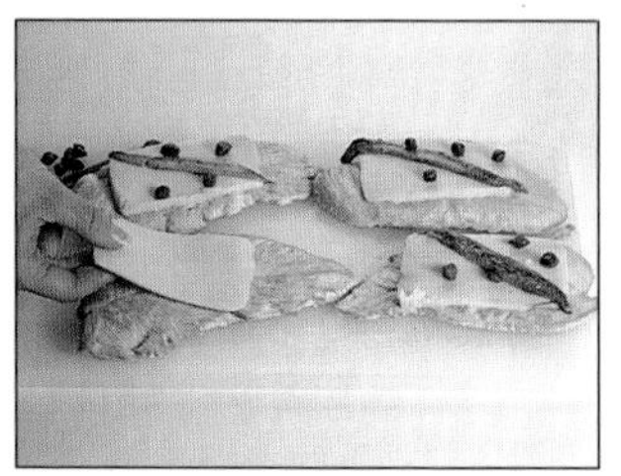

Step 3 Place a slice of cheese on top of each turkey scallop and top with anchovies, capers, and herbs.

3. Drain the anchovy fillets and rinse them well. Dry on kitchen paper. Place a slice of cheese on top of each turkey fillet and arrange the anchovies and capers on top of each. Sprinkle with the herbs and return to the skillet.

4. Cook the meat a further 5 minutes over moderate heat until the turkey is cooked through and the cheese has melted. Remove to a serving platter and keep warm.

5. Return the pan to the heat and add the Marsala to deglaze, then reduce the heat. Add the cream and whisk in well. Simmer gently, uncovered, for a few minutes to thicken the sauce. Season with salt and pepper and spoon the sauce over the turkey to serve.

Vegetable Risotto

SERVES 4

Risotto is a highly adaptable and ever popular rice dish; try this vegetable version as a change from the everyday chicken variety.

PREPARATION: 15 mins
COOKING: 30 mins

2 large leaves Swiss chard (silverbeet)
2 tbsps butter
½ onion, minced
1 carrot, diced
1 stick celery, diced
2 cups rice, uncooked
⅔ cup frozen peas
1 thick slice ham, diced
Salt and pepper

1. Cut the green leaf part of the chard into very thin strips, then cut the white stalk into small dice.

2. Heat the butter in a large skillet and fry the onion, carrot, celery, and the green parts and white parts of the chard 2 minutes.

3. Add the rice, peas, and ham to the skillet, stir well, and cook until the rice is transparent.

4. Transfer to an ovenproof dish and add 3 cups boiling water. Season with salt and pepper and stir well.

Step 1 Cut the green leaf part of the chard into very thin strips.

Step 1 Cut the white stalks of the chard into small dice.

5. Cover the dish and cook in a preheated 400°F oven, for between 18 and 20 minutes. Serve hot.

Sicilian Caponata

SERVES 6

Vegetables, so important in Italian cuisine, are often served separately. This combination makes an excellent vegetable entrée, side-dish or appetizer.

PREPARATION: 35 mins
COOKING: 30 mins

1 large eggplant
Salt
⅔ cup olive oil
1 onion, sliced
2 red bell peppers, cut into 1-inch pieces
2 sticks celery, sliced thickly
4 cups canned plum tomatoes
2 tbsps red wine vinegar
1 tbsp sugar
1 clove garlic, crushed
Salt and pepper
12 black olives
1 tbsp capers

1. Cut the eggplant in half and score the cut surface. Sprinkle with salt and leave to drain in a colander or on kitchen paper for 30 minutes.

Step 1 Halve the eggplant and score the cut surface. Sprinkle with salt and leave to drain.

Step 4 Roll the olives on a flat surface to loosen the stones.

Rinse, pat dry, and cut into 1-inch cubes.

2. Heat the oil in a large skillet and add the onion, peppers, and celery. Cook gently 5 minutes, stirring occasionally. Add the eggplant and cook a further 5 minutes.

3. Sieve the tomatoes to remove the seeds and add the pulp and liquid to the pan. Add the remaining ingredients, except the olives and capers, and cook a further 2 minutes.

4. To pit the olives, roll them on a flat surface to loosen the stones and then remove them with a swivel vegetable peeler or a cherry pitter. Slice into quarters and add to the vegetables with the capers.

5. Simmer, uncovered, over a moderate heat for 15 minutes to allow most of the liquid to evaporate. Adjust the seasoning and serve hot or cold.

Apple Fritters

SERVES 4

A simple dessert that is always popular. Either dredge with sugar or serve with a fresh fruit coulis.

PREPARATION: 15 mins
COOKING: 20 mins

---

2 dessert apples, peeled, cored, and cut into small pieces
½ cup orange juice
¼ cup Marsala
2 cups sifted all-purpose flour
¼ tsp baking powder
2 tbsps ground almonds
½ cup milk
2 egg yolks
2 tbsps sugar
Oil for deep frying

---

1. Marinate the apple in the orange juice and the Marsala 15 minutes.

2. Mix together the flour, baking powder, and the ground almonds.

3. Whisk together the sugar and egg yolks until pale and thick.

Step 4 Stir the milk into the mixture and beat very well.

4. Beat together the egg mixture and the flour mixture. Stir in the milk and beat really well.

5. Add the flour and egg mixture to the apples in their marinade. Stir gently to blend the ingredients together evenly. Allow to rest 10 minutes.

6. Heat the oil and gently add tablespoons of apple and fritter mixture. When each fritter has cooked through and turned golden brown, remove with a slotted spoon.

7. Drain on kitchen paper and serve either hot or cold.

Amarena Ice Cream

SERVES 4

Amarena is an Italian variety of plum-colored cherry. Cherries make the most delicious flavoring for ice cream.

PREPARATION: 30 mins
FREEZING: 30 mins–1 hour

2¼ cups milk
6 egg yolks
4 tbsps sugar
4 tbsps canned cherries (Amarena if possible) in their juice, coarsely chopped

1. Whisk together the egg yolks and the sugar until the mixture is pale and creamy.

2. Bring the milk almost to the boil and beat it into the egg mixture.

3. Return the custard mixture to the pan, reduce the heat to low, and cook, beating continuously, until the mixture thickens enough to coat the back of a spoon.

Step 2 Whisk the scalded milk into the egg mixture.

Step 3 Cook the custard mixture over a gentle heat, until it thickens enough to coat the back of a spoon.

4. Remove from the heat and stir in the chopped cherries and their juice. Allow to cool.

5. Pour the custard into the bowl of an ice cream maker and set in motion.*

6. When the ice cream has crystallized, spoon into a container and keep in the freezer until needed.

* If an ice cream maker is not available, pour the mixture into a shallow freezer tray and place in the refrigerator freezer until partially frozen. Remove the tray from the freezer and beat the mixture to break up the crystals. Refreeze, beat thoroughly again, and pour into a covered container. Freeze until firm.

Black Cherry Ravioli with Sour Cream Sauce

SERVES 4

This dessert is a wonderful contrast of colors and flavors.

PREPARATION: 35 mins
COOKING: 15 mins

Dough
2 cups all-purpose flour
1 tbsp sugar
3 eggs

1 Large can black pitted cherries, juice reserved
2 tbsps sugar
1 tsp cornstarch
½ cup sour cream
½ cup heavy cream

1. Put cherries in a sieve. Strain off the juice and reserve.

2. Make the dough by sifting the flour and sugar into a bowl. Make a well in the center and add the lightly-beaten eggs. Work the flour and eggs together with a spoon, and then by hand, until a smooth dough is formed. Knead gently.

3. Lightly flour a board, and roll the dough out thinly into a rectangle. Cut the dough in half.

4. Put the well-drained cherries about 1½-inches apart on one dough rectangle. Place the other dough rectangle on top, and cut with a small glass or cookie cutter. Seal well around the edges with the back of a fork.

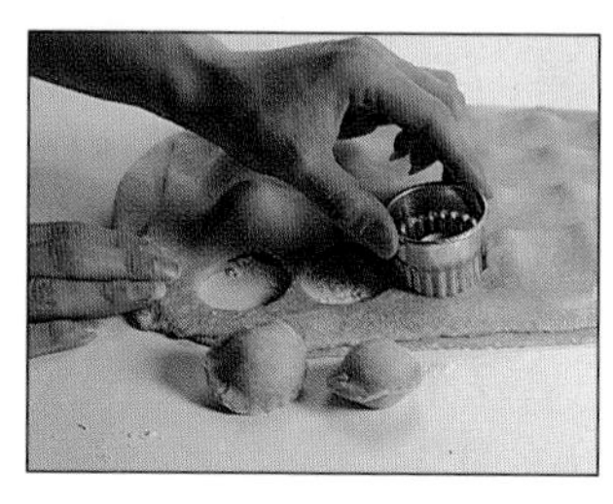

Step 4 Cut the pasta with a cookie cutter.

5. Boil plenty of water in a large saucepan, and drop the cherry pasta into it, a few at a time. Cook for about 10 minutes, or until they rise to the surface. Remove with a slotted spoon and keep warm.

6. Mix 1 tablespoon of the reserved cherry juice with the cornstarch. Mix the remaining juice with the sugar and set over the heat. Add the cornstarch mixture, and heat, stirring until it thickens.

7. Meanwhile mix the sour cream and heavy cream together and marble 1 tablespoon of cherry juice through it.

8. Pour the hot, thickened cherry juice over cherry ravioli. Serve hot with the marbled cream sauce.

Index

ECOSYSTEMS OF THE WORLD

GRASSLAND ECOSYSTEMS

by Melissa Higgins

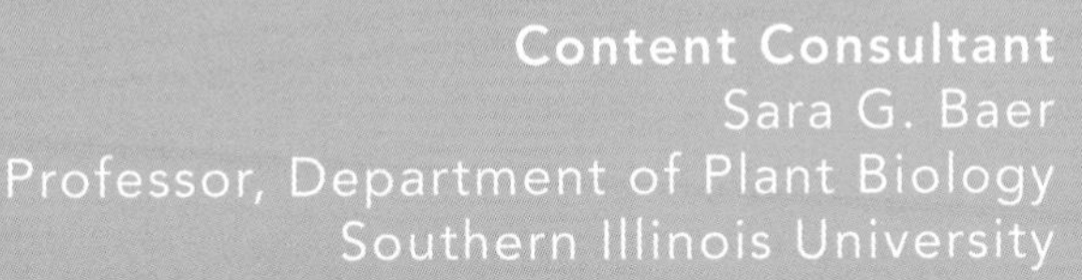

Content Consultant
Sara G. Baer
Professor, Department of Plant Biology
Southern Illinois University

An Imprint of Abdo Publishing
abdopublishing.com

abdopublishing.com

Published by Abdo Publishing, a division of ABDO, PO Box 398166, Minneapolis, Minnesota 55439.

Printed in the United States of America, North Mankato, Minnesota
042015
092015

Cover Photo: iStockphoto
Interior Photos: iStockphoto, 1, 4, 8, 22, 24 (top), 24 (top right), 24 (middle), 24 (bottom left), 24 (bottom right), 26, 31, 34, 40, 43, 45; Shutterstock Images, 10, 24 (middle top), 28; Steve Geer/iStockphoto, 14; Suzanne Tucker/Shutterstock Images, 16; Lynn Bystrom/iStockphoto, 19; Jason R. Warren/iStockphoto, 24 (top left); James Tung/iStockphoto, 36; Chris Crafter/iStockphoto, 38

Editor: Jon Westmark
Series Designer: Becky Daum

Library of Congress Control Number: 2015931039

Cataloging-in-Publication Data
Higgins, Melissa.
Grassland ecosystems / Melissa Higgins.
p. cm. -- (Ecosystems of the world)
Includes bibliographical references and index.
ISBN 978-1-62403-854-9
1. Grassland ecology--Juvenile literature. 2. Grasslands--Juvenile literature.
I. Title.
577.4--dc23

2015931039

CONTENTS

CHAPTER ONE

WHAT IS A GRASSLAND?

A mouse hurries through dry stalks of grass. It is looking for its favorite seeds. A hawk coasts overhead looking for its favorite meal—the mouse. The hawk dives to the ground. It snatches the mouse in its claws and flies away. The hawk carries the mouse to its hungry chicks.

Thousands of miles away, a lightning bolt hits dry grass. Flames shoot across the countryside. Gazelles,

Red-tailed hawks circle over grasslands looking for movement on the ground.

hedgehogs, and cranes scurry or fly to safety. Underground, grass roots are not harmed. They will spring new growth when rain comes.

Around the World

Grasslands exist on every continent except Antarctica. This ecosystem covers approximately 40 percent of Earth's land surface. All of the grasslands in the world have one thing in common—grass is their most common plant.

Grasslands are known by different names around the world. In North America, most grasslands are called Great Plains. In Africa they are known as savannas or velds. Most grasslands in Eastern Europe and Asia are called steppes. Grasslands in South America are

And the Winner Is . . .

Australia is the country with the biggest percentage of land covered with grasslands. Approximately 70 percent of Australia is grasslands. Forty-two percent of China is covered with grasslands. Grasslands cover 37 percent of Russia, 36 percent of the United States, and 32 percent of Canada.

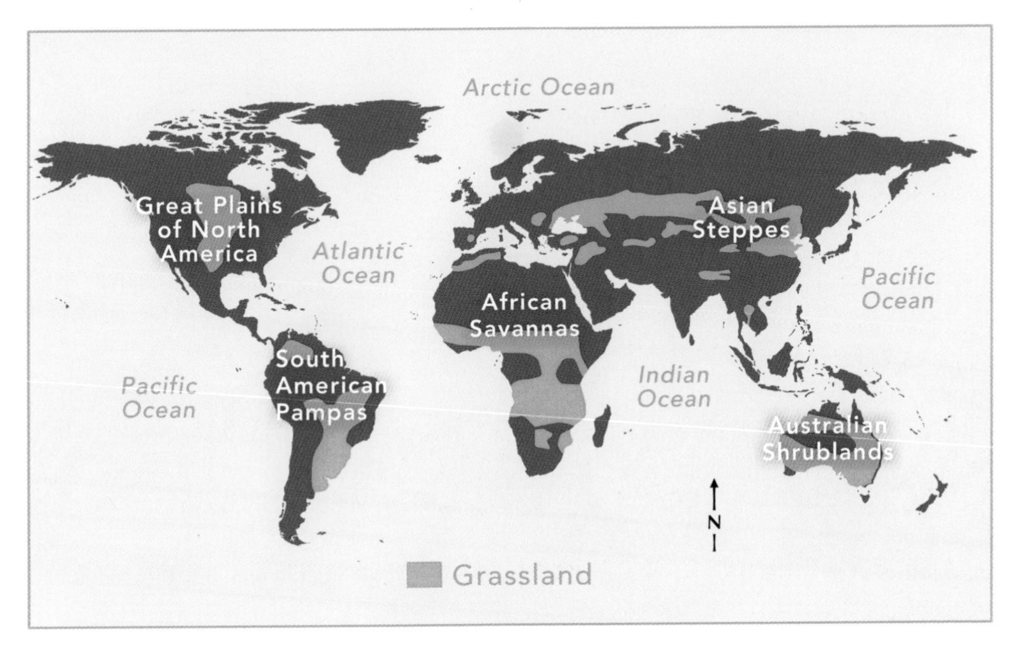

Grasslands of the World
This map shows grasslands across the world. Sometimes a picture is easier to understand than reading words. In two sentences, explain if looking at this map or reading the text of Chapter One helps you better understand where grasslands are located.

called pampas, llanos, or cerrados. Most Australian grasslands are known as shrublands.

Grasslands are diverse ecosystems. This means they contain many different kinds of plants and animals. Some of the biggest animals on the planet live in grasslands. Grasslands contain hundreds of types of grasses and other plants, such as wildflowers. A healthy grassland ecosystem contains a delicate

African elephants are the world's largest land animals. Habitat loss is one reason they are endangered.

balance between its plants, animals, and the environment.

Important Yesterday and Today

In the past, many grasslands were larger and had more wild animals than they do today. Over time, people began to grow crops. They also learned how to raise animals for food. Farming and grazing took over much of the world's grasslands. Many other grasslands were destroyed when towns and cities were built on them.

But grasslands continue to be important ecosystems. Land that was once grassland is now farmland that provides food for much of the world. Surviving grasslands attract tourists and are used for recreation. Grasslands help limit global warming. They are one of the most important ecosystems on Earth.

Helping the Environment

Factories and automobiles put a large amount of a gas called carbon dioxide into the air. Like the glass covering a greenhouse, carbon dioxide traps heat. This makes the world warmer. Grasslands help fight global warming. Grassland plants take up carbon dioxide into their leaves and use it to make roots. This removes the gas from the air. Scientists are looking for ways to make grassland plants store even more carbon dioxide.

CHAPTER TWO

GRASSLAND CLIMATE AND WEATHER

Grasslands can be divided into two main types: tropical and temperate. Most tropical grasslands are located in the southern hemisphere. They cover large areas of Africa, South America, and Australia. Temperate grasslands are found mostly in the northern hemisphere in North America and Eurasia.

Maned wolves have long legs that help them see over the tall grass of tropical cerrados.

Scientists also sort grasslands by how much moisture is in the air. A lack of moisture is called aridity. Scientists classify grasslands using six aridity zones: cold (the driest zone), hyperarid, arid, semiarid, dry subhumid, and humid.

Tropical grasslands are mostly semiarid or humid. Summer brings 28 to 56 inches (71–142 cm) of rain to tropical grasslands. The grasses in these areas can grow very tall because they get so much rain. Some grow up to seven feet (2 m) tall. The dry season lasts for two to seven months. Tropical grasslands do not get much colder than 64 degrees Fahrenheit (18°C), even in the dry winter months.

Rain Shadows

A rain shadow is an area of very dry land that is blocked from moisture by a mountain range. Rain shadows can create dry grasslands. The western portion of the Great Plains in the United States sits in the rain shadow of the Rocky Mountains. As a result, this region only supports shorter grasses.

Temperate grasslands are mostly arid and

semiarid. Rainfall ranges from 10 to 30 inches (25–100 cm) per year in these areas. Grasses in the temperate region tend to be shorter because they get less rain than tropical grasslands. The driest temperate grasslands are the western short-grass prairies of the United States and Canada. The tallgrass prairies in the eastern parts of these two countries get more rain. Grasses here can grow very tall if they are not grazed. Temperatures in temperate grasslands can vary from below freezing in winter to more than 100 degrees Fahrenheit (38°C) in summer.

EXPLORE ONLINE

The focus of Chapter Two is the climate and temperature of grasslands. The website also discusses these things. As you know, every source is different. What information on the website is the same as the information in Chapter Two? What are the differences? What else can you learn about grasslands from the website?

The Grassland Biome

mycorelibrary.com/grassland-ecosystems

GRASSLAND PLANTS

Plants play an important role in grasslands. Grasses have a large root system that anchors them to the ground. This keeps the soil in place. When plants die and decay, they return nutrients to the soil. This makes the soil richer. Plants also bring energy into the ecosystem. They combine the energy from sunlight with carbon dioxide and water to make sugar. Sugar provides food for plants to grow. This

Prairie sunflowers turn to follow the sun to take in more light.

Forbs are common in grasslands. They often have colorful flowers.

process is known as photosynthesis. When an animal eats a plant, the plant's energy transfers to the animal. This allows the animal to grow.

Native Plants

The most common plant in grasslands is grass. But grasslands can contain hundreds of different plant species. There are approximately 10,000 types of grass in the world today. In the United States, common prairie grasses include blue grama, big bluestem, wheatgrass, and buffalo grass. All grasses have slender leaves, called blades.

Sedges, rushes, and other grasslike plants grow in grasslands. Forbs and a few types of woody plants can also grow in grasslands. Forbs tend to have wider leaves than grass and often produce showy flowers. Forbs include globe mallow, sunflower, coneflower, and black-eyed Susan. Trees and shrubs are woody plants. Not many woody plants are found in healthy grasslands. Fires are common in thriving grasslands. The blazes burn woody plants before they can grow too large.

Buffalo Grass

Buffalo grass is one of the most important plants of the US short-grass prairie. Pronghorn, rabbits, and prairie dogs graze on it. It was once the main source of food for the huge herds of bison that roamed the prairie. The burs on buffalo grass seeds cling to animal fur. They drop off the animal in new places and grow into plants. Buffalo grass roots can grow five feet (1.5 m) deep in the soil. The grass is resistant to heat and cold because of its deep root system.

Grassland plants have adapted to grow well in their environment. Grasses and forbs have developed deep roots. These roots are not harmed by fire and can reach moisture deep underground. Grasses' long, slender leaves have a small area for the sun to shine on. This keeps them from losing too much water. Forbs hold their broad leaves upright to avoid too much sunlight. Both grasses and forbs have low growing points. This means that the part of the plant that makes new cells is close to the ground, protected from grazing animals. Many

More Plant Species than the Tropics

Tropical ecosystems have more plant species across large areas than any other ecosystem—as many as 942 plant species per 2.5 acres (1 ha). But in 2012, a team of biologists measured the number of plants in smaller spaces. In these places, grasslands had more plant species than any other ecosystem. A 527-square-foot (49-sq-m) patch of grassland in the Czech Republic contained 131 plant species. A 10-square-foot (0.1-sq-m) area of grassland in Romania had 43 plant species.

Some nonnative species, such as Canada thistle, spread their seeds by sticking to animals and people.

grassland plants can go dormant. This helps them survive harsh conditions.

Nonnative Plants

Plants introduced to an ecosystem where they do not usually grow are called nonnative plants. These plants might be brought to an area accidentally. They can be carried by wind, animals, or people. Nonnative plants are not often affected by the same weather conditions, diseases, and insects that help keep native plants in check. So nonnative plants can quickly overtake a natural grassland habitat. One study looked at plants in the Pawnee National Grasslands in eastern Colorado. Out of 410 plants, 70 were nonnative. These plants take space and resources away from native plants.

Humans may bring nonnative plants to an area for a specific reason, such as for farming. Rich soils make grasslands some of the best farmlands on Earth. Grasslands tend be flat. This makes them easy to farm. Many parts of the world that were once native grasslands are now used for growing food. The US prairie, for example, is one of the richest farming regions on Earth. Crops, such as corn, soybeans, cotton, and wheat, have replaced many native grassland plants in the United States.

Fire and Grazing

Fire, both natural and man-made, is important to grasslands. Fires destroy trees and shrubs that might overtake grasslands. Fire burns away layers of dead plant material. This provides more light for grassland plants to regrow.

Grazing animals are also important to grasslands. Like fire, grazing opens up areas of soil to more light. It reduces the height and density of grasses, making room for shorter plants to grow. This can help grasslands become more diverse. But grazing can be harmful to native plants. If animals are kept in a single area for too long, they can eat too much of the grass. Overgrazing hurts plant and soil health because plants do not have a chance to fully grow. This can open up areas for nonnative plants to enter.

FURTHER EVIDENCE

Chapter Three provides information about grassland plants and some of the factors that help and hinder healthy grasslands. What was one of the chapter's main points? Go to the website below. Find a quote from the website that supports one of the chapter's main points. Does the quote support an existing piece of evidence, or does it add a new one?

Grassland Ecosystems Profile

mycorelibrary.com/grassland-ecosystems

CHAPTER FOUR

GRASSLAND ANIMALS

Animals are important to grasslands in many ways. Prairie dogs, for example, prune the plants they eat. Their droppings make the soil more fertile. Their burrows provide homes for many other small animals. And small animals provide food for grassland predators.

In the past, grasslands stretched unbroken for hundreds of miles. There were herds of millions

Prairie dog holes provide shelter for other burrowing animals and make the soil more fertile.

Grassland Food Web
This illustration shows a typical grassland food web. The arrows show the movement of energy through the ecosystem. In what ways is the information in the diagram the same or different from the information described in Chapter Four?

of wild animals. There are fewer wild animals in grasslands today. In some areas, food crops are planted where wild grasses once grew. Domesticated animals compete with wild animals for food and space. But grassland animals are still as diverse and interesting as those found in any ecosystem.

Grazers and Predators

Some grassland animals eat only plants. They are called herbivores. These animals take in energy plants have created through photosynthesis. Examples of tropical grassland herbivores are elephants, gazelles, zebras, and giraffes. Antelope, bison, jackrabbits, and prairie dogs are herbivores that live in temperate grasslands.

The Last Bison

Scientists estimate that up to 30 million bison once roamed the Great Plains. In the early to mid-1800s, the governments of Canada and the United States decided to develop the Great Plains for farming and ranching. This decision led to the mass killing of bison. The animal was almost wiped out. The last free-roaming bison were killed in the United States in 1891. Bison today live in nature preserves, parks, and zoos, as well as on private land.

Monarch caterpillars eat milkweed for approximately two weeks until they are fully grown. They then begin the process of becoming a butterfly.

Some animals eat only meat. They are called carnivores. Lions, hyenas, leopards, and cheetahs are carnivores in tropical grasslands. Bobcats, wolves, snakes, owls, and hawks are carnivores in temperate grasslands.

Omnivores eat both plants and other animals. Jackals, warthogs, ostriches, and baboons are omnivores in tropical grasslands. Temperate grasslands are home to omnivores such as raccoons, coyotes, foxes, and various bird species.

Insects

Insects are the most abundant and diverse group of animals in grasslands. Insects are very important to grasslands. Some insects, such as bees, pollinate plants. This allows plants to make seeds that grow into new plants. Other insects, such as dung beetles, help break down dead plant and animal material. This creates rich soil for plants and helps clear the ground for new growth. Grasslands, in turn, provide a home for insects to thrive. Grasshoppers, bees, beetles, and ants live in both tropical and temperate grasslands. These insects provide food for many birds and small mammals.

All grassland animals play a part in this ecosystem. They each help balance the system to ensure its continuing survival.

Butterfly and Milkweed

Two natives of the prairie, the monarch butterfly and the milkweed plant, depend on each other. Milkweed produces a bad-tasting poison that keeps most insects from eating it. But the poison does not hurt the monarch. When it is a caterpillar, the monarch eats only milkweed. The poison builds up in its body. This makes the caterpillar poisonous to birds. In turn the butterfly pollinates the milkweed. This helps ensure its survival.

CHAPTER FIVE

PEOPLE AND GRASSLANDS

People have lived in grassland ecosystems throughout human history. In fact the earliest people may have lived on African savannas. Over time, human activity has changed grasslands. But people today still depend on grasslands for their food and livelihood.

Many people still rely on grasslands to feed their herds of animals.

Fragmented Grasslands

Fragmentation happens when a large ecosystem is separated into small sections. People split up grasslands by building roads and cities, as well as planting crops. Fragmentation makes it harder for fire to spread. It also makes more edges. Edges are places where grasslands border other types of land. Edges can let trees, shrubs, and nonnative species find their way onto grasslands. Native grassland animals have a harder time finding mates and food in small grassland patches. Fragmentation can lead plants and animals to go extinct.

Spears to Plows

Early humans gathered native grassland plants for food and medicine. They hunted large grazing animals, eating their meat and using their hides for clothing and shelter. Hunters knew they had better chances of finding game on healthier grasslands. They set fire to grasslands to keep them free of shrubs and trees. Burning also extended grasslands into larger areas.

Approximately 11,000 years ago, humans began to grow crops from grass

Land fragmentation and farming hurt grassland habitats.

grains. They started raising cattle for food. Humans eventually began to rely less on hunting and gathering and more on farming. This change reduced grasslands all over the world. People plowed grasslands to grow crops. Tamed animals were kept in small areas, where they overgrazed grasslands.

With an abundance of food produced with the help of grassland soil, the human population grew. People built towns and cities on grasslands. They began preventing fires instead of using fires to manage grasslands. Large grasslands were split into smaller sections. Animals that needed larger habitats could not survive in these smaller areas. Their populations fell.

People and Grasslands Today

People still depend on grasslands today. They eat meat and dairy products from animals raised on grasslands. People hunt native grassland animals for food. Crops, such as wheat, corn, and soybeans, are grown on grasslands. They are used to feed most of the people of the world.

Grasslands provide other opportunities, such as hiking, hunting, and nature viewing. For example, tourists enjoy seeing the elephants, lions, and giraffes of the African savanna. Tourism can help visitors understand and respect grasslands.

Some people use grasslands as their ancestors did. On the Mongolian steppe, for example, early people moved their sheep and yak herds around grasslands for good grazing. Some people living in this part of the world still do this today.

STRAIGHT TO THE SOURCE

This US Geological Survey (USGS) press release from 2001 discusses the dangers fragmented grasslands pose to nesting birds:

> *As grassland areas are divided into smaller tracts of land, there are more "edges" and fewer large, open grassland areas for birds to nest in. . . . From 1998 through 2000, USGS biologist Rosalind Renfrew and her colleagues . . . placed miniature cameras at 89 nests of five grassland bird species in southwestern Wisconsin pastures. They found that most of the bird predators were raccoons, thirteen-lined ground squirrels, and snakes. About one-third of the nest failures were caused by species that prefer the woody edges of grasslands, such as raccoons and opossums, and these nests were usually closer to woody edges than other types of edges.*

Source: Rebecca Phipps. "Grassland Birds and Habitat Fragmentation: The Role of Predators." USGS Newsroom. *US Geological Survey, August 5, 2001. Web. Accessed February 24, 2015.*

What's the Big Idea?

Take a close look at this passage. What is the main connection being made between land fragmentation and bird population? What can you tell about the relationship between bird nests and grassland edges?

CHAPTER SIX

THE FUTURE OF GRASSLANDS

All of the parts of a healthy grassland ecosystem support one another. So problems with one part can cause problems with others. For example, a sudden loss of coyotes or badgers due to overhunting could cause the number of prairie dogs to rise. When there are too many prairie dogs, grassland plants may be overgrazed. Having fewer plants could cause soil to erode and weeds to spread.

Coyotes help control the population of burrowing animals, such as prairie dogs.

As human populations grow, more grasslands are being developed for human use.

There are many threats to the world's grasslands. Most threats are a result of human activity, such as urban growth. Urban areas continue to cut into grasslands. But humans are taking action to save these important ecosystems.

Threats to Grasslands

Crop production is one of the biggest threats to native grasslands. Native grasslands are continually being converted to farmland. Poor farming methods, such as growing only one type of crop year after year on the same soil, increase the chances of pests and disease. Pests and disease increase the need for chemicals and substances that protect crops. These things can be toxic to native plants and wildlife.

Nonnative animals threaten native grasslands. Cattle can harm grasslands if there are too many of the animals in too small of an area. They overgraze and erode the soil. Nonnative plants may grow in overgrazed areas. Once nonnative plants start growing, they quickly reproduce and compete with native plants. Nonnative plants are often not as nutritious as native plants. As a result, native grassland animals have a harder time thriving.

Black-Footed Ferrets

The black-footed ferret is a type of weasel native to the Great Plains. It was once thought to be extinct. Over the past 30 years, state governments, federal agencies, zoos, conservation groups, Native-American tribes, and landowners have helped bring the ferret back to its native grasslands. Today there are almost 1,000 black-footed ferrets in North America. The animal is still endangered. But its recovery shows that the prairies where it lives are healthy.

Habitat loss and hunting have hurt African lion numbers.

There are other threats to grasslands too. One example is climate change. Climate change can vary the amount of rainfall an area receives. Too much rain can cause flooding and erosion in grasslands.

Fire suppression is another concern for grasslands. For a long time, people have tried to stop the spread of fire in these ecosystems. As a result, trees and shrubs have taken over some grasslands.

Because of hunting, there are fewer big grazing animals, such as elephants and zebras, living on the

African grasslands. Hunting also has reduced the number of predators, such as lions and cheetahs.

Helping Grasslands

People are taking action to preserve grasslands. This can be as simple as getting rid of trees and shrubs and setting fires in the dry season. Some areas need more work. This might include planting native seeds and reintroducing native animals.

Establishing national parks helps protect grasslands. Two grassland national parks include Theodore Roosevelt National Park in North Dakota and Grasslands National Park in Saskatchewan, Canada.

Many countries have passed laws against hunting endangered

Biofuel

Some native grasses are being used in Europe and North America as an energy source. Switchgrass, buffalo grass, tall fescue, and canary grass can be grown in poor soil. These grasses are changed into a liquid fuel. The fuel can be used to make heat and electricity. It also can be used in place of gasoline for some cars and trucks.

One way people help protect grasslands is by starting and controlling fires.

animals. Farmers help grasslands by letting soil rest between planting crops or by restoring grasslands on formerly cultivated soil. Ranchers help grasslands by moving their livestock to new locations to keep them from overgrazing.

In the past, people often protected grasslands. In return, grasslands provided them with food, clothing, and shelter. Today people are beginning to understand grasslands are too valuable to lose. They are trying to find new ways to protect them.

STRAIGHT TO THE SOURCE

President Theodore Roosevelt began as a rancher in North Dakota in the 1880s. During that time, he witnessed the prairie grasslands being ruined. He created the US Forest Service to protect wildlife. In his 1913 article "Our Vanishing Wild Life," he wrote:

> *[I]t is also vandalism wantonly to destroy or permit the destruction of what is beautiful in nature, whether it be a cliff, a forest, or a species of mammal or bird. Here in the United States we turn our rivers and streams into sewers and dumping-grounds, we pollute the air, we destroy forests, and exterminate fishes, birds and mammals—not to speak of vulgarizing charming landscapes with hideous advertisements. But at last it looks as if our people were awakening.*

Source: Theodore Roosevelt. "Our Vanishing Wild Life."
Theodore Roosevelt and Conservation. *National Park Service, February 22, 2015.*
Web. Accessed February 24, 2015.

Back It Up

Roosevelt used harsh words to describe what was being done to the environment. But he ended his article on a note of hope. Write a paragraph describing at least three pieces of evidence from Chapter Six showing how countries can help grassland plants and animals.

WELL-KNOWN GRASSLANDS

Great Plains of North America

The Great Plains of North America are located in the United States and Canada. Almost 90 percent of this temperate grassland ecosystem has been converted to farmland and cities. This is more than any other grasslands in the world. Some of the best-known mammals of the Great Plains of North America are bison, coyotes, and prairie dogs.

South American Pampas, Llanos, and Cerrados

The South American grasslands are located in the southern half of South America. They are found in Argentina, Brazil, Bolivia, Paraguay, Uruguay, and a small part of Chile. More than 75 percent of the South American tropical grasslands are now used for farming and ranching. Jaguars, maned wolves, giant armadillos, and giant anteaters live here.

Central Eurasian Steppes

The temperate steppes range from northeastern China westward through parts of Russia to the Ural Mountains. Only about 20 percent of this grassland ecosystem has been converted to cities and farmland. Wild animals, such as the Mongolian gazelle, hedgehogs, marmots, and several species of crane, share the land with domesticated sheep, yaks, and goats.

The shape of their feet enables the kangaroos of the Australian shrubland to move around by hopping.

African Savannas

The African savanna spreads through 27 countries. More than 73 percent of these grasslands still remain. The savannas are home to some of the best-known animals on the planet. Elephants, giraffes, lions, zebras, rhinoceros, and wildebeest call this ecosystem home. One of the world's most famous national parks, the Serengeti, has the largest number of wild grazing animals and predators in Africa.

Australian Shrubland

Australia has more of its land covered in grasslands than any other continent. Approximately 57 percent of its grasslands have not been converted to cities or farmland. Australia does not have large herds of animals as Africa does. But kangaroos, wallabies, dingos, wild pigs, ravens, eagles, and rabbits all live on Australia's shrubland.

STOP AND THINK

Take a Stand

This book explores how some grasslands are being lost to agriculture. Which do you think is more important, preserving grasslands or expanding farmland? Or do you think both are important? Write a short essay explaining your opinion. Make sure to give reasons for your opinion and facts and details to support those reasons.

Tell the Tale

Chapter Five discusses the first humans who lived in grasslands. Write 200 words telling the story of a hunter living on the Great Plains of North America 2,000 years ago. What animal species does he hunt? What types of plants does he gather? What is the hunter thinking about? Describe the sights and sounds of the grasslands. Be sure to set the scene, develop a sequence of events, and offer a conclusion.

Why Do I Care?

Think about the foods you eat and the clothes you wear. How many of them come from plants or animals that live in grassland ecosystems? What if grassland plants and animals no longer existed? How would your life be different? Are there things you would miss? What are they?

Surprise Me

Think about what you learned from this book. Which two or three facts did you find most surprising? Write a short paragraph about each fact describing what you found surprising and why.

GLOSSARY

adaption
a change in a population over time

aridity
a measure of how much an area lacks moisture

diverse
showing a great deal of variety

domesticated
tamed or grown by humans

dormant
not actively growing but able to begin growing again

endangered
in danger of becoming extinct

extinct
no longer existing

forb
a flowering herb

graze
to eat small amounts of food throughout the day

sedge
a grass-like plant that grows in wet ground or near water

species
a group of living beings that are similar to one another

LEARN MORE

Books

Latham, Donna. *Savannas and Grasslands*. White River Junction, VT: Nomad Press, 2011.

Patkau, Karen. *Who Needs a Prairie? A Grassland Ecosystem*. Toronto: Tundra Books, 2014.

Roumanis, Alexis. *Grasslands*. New York: AV2 by Weigl, 2015.

Websites

To learn more about Ecosystems of the World, visit **booklinks.abdopublishing.com**. These links are routinely monitored and updated to provide the most current information available.

Visit **mycorelibrary.com** for free additional tools for teachers and students.

INDEX

ABOUT THE AUTHOR

Melissa Higgins writes fiction and nonfiction for children and young adults. When she's not writing, Higgins enjoys hiking and taking photographs in the Arizona desert, where she lives with her husband.